My thanks to the German Tea Association, accessed on
the Internet through a highly professional homepage at
www.teeverband.de, where you can learn anything and
everything you ever wanted to know about tea. Other
great resources about tea include The Tea Council
www.teacouncil.co.uk, and Planet Tea www.planet-tea.com.

Design: Niels Bonnemeier
Production: Patty Holden
Editors: Monika Römer, Gabriele Heßmann, Lisa M. Tooker
Food Editor: Lynda Zuber Sassi
Translation: Christie Tam
©2003 Verlag W. Hölker GmbH, Münster
English translation for the U.S. market
©2006 Silverback Books, Inc.
ISBN: 1-59637-074-2
Printed in China

Rose Marie Donhauser

Little

Tea Book

Contents

Unless otherwise indicated, all recipes make four servings.

Introduction

"We drink tea to forget the noise of the world."
—T'ien Yi-heng

More writing and philosophizing has focused on tea than any other luxury item in the world. In its 3000-year history, much has been reported about customs and usages, the art of cultivating, and blending different varieties, and, above all, tea's expert handling and loving preparation. Poets and thinkers have always been and continue to be inspired by tea and are literally, stimulated by it.

Tea is the prepared leaf from the tea bush or tea plant. Tea has been cultivated for thousands of years in Asia. It was originally used in China as a medicinal herb. The first evidence of tea being consumed for pleasure was in the 6th century AD. The tea ceremony did not become popular in Japan until the 16th century. The Dutch imported the first Chinese tea to Europe, followed by the English, whose famous "tea time" has been an important part of British culture since the 17th century. Although tea became a favorite drink in Europe, the drink never assumed the same degree of importance as it enjoys in Asian countries.

Personally, I have very fond memories of tea. As a teenager and young adult, I took many trips to England. Each host family with whom I would stay had their own tea tradition. Usually, the mother would bring the perfect cup of tea to my room each morning. The tea would be at the ideal temperature, briefly steeped and mixed with milk and a little sugar. The thought of this flavor sensation today makes my mouth water.

Since that time, I've spent many mornings attempting to re-create that perfect cup of tea to no avail. While my tea is quite good, I've never been able to replicate the flavor from the memories of my younger days. Perhaps it's the water. Along with the quality of the tea itself, the quality of the water is one of the secrets in making the perfect cup of tea.

With this little book, I would like to teach you something about fermented (black) and unfermented (green) tea. To do so, I'll give you a more detailed history of tea and guide you through the jungle of technical terms. I will describe how good tea is made and how to know which equipment and method of preparation will deliver the most authentic flavor. Above all, however, I will share a lot of fine recipes.

I'll leave you with a quote from the English statesman William Gladstone and wish you lot's of fun reading this book and enjoying your tea: "If you are cold, tea will warm you; if you are depressed it will cheer you; if you are excited it will calm you."

History, Anecdotes and Interesting Facts

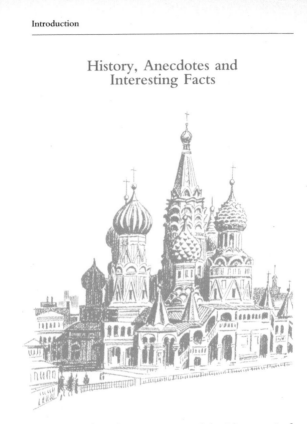

Many legends and stories surround the "discovery" of the tea plant. According to the oldest Chinese writings, Emperor Chen Nung (2737–2679) was its original discoverer. During his reign, he concentrated on its healing powers, but one day, a tea leaf accidentally fell into his cooking pot. Beguiled by its effect and aroma, he carefully examined the tea plant. Thus began tea's holistic career in China. According to a tradition dating back to the late Han Dynasty (25–221 AD), the Chinese scholar Gan Lu brought tea seeds back to China from one of his many trips to India. By this time, however, the Chinese were supposedly already convinced of the tea plant's healing powers.

A Buddhist legend tells the story of a Bodhi-Dharma who was too tired to stay awake during meditation. His solution was to cut off his eyelids and bury them in the ground. They miraculously took root and grew into a tea bush.

Naturally, India prefers its own legend about the origins of tea. While meditating, the Fakir Dharma had the following experience: He wanted to demonstrate his Buddhist faith by staying awake and meditating for seven years. He sat under a bush and whenever he was overcome by fatigue, he placed some of the loose leaves from this bush in his mouth and stayed awake by chewing them. Thanks to the plant's stimulating quality, he was able to achieve his goal.

And, of course, there's "Asterix in Britain," where Goscinny and Uderzo tell their own unique story of how the British got their tea (see page 22).

Cultivation of a Wild Plant

The way we drink tea today has little to do with its beginnings. Centuries after the discovery of the tea plant, tea was used strictly for medicinal purposes. The bushes growing wild were 13–16 feet high and yielded very little. Although it was known that from 200–100 BC, the emperors of the Chinese Han Dynasty cultivated tea plants in the palace gardens, tea did not become a popular Chinese drink until the 7th Century AD. Giant tea gardens were established throughout China, in bordering Tibet and in Japan.

Around 800 AD, the Chinese author Lu Yu, who supposedly grew up as an orphan in a Buddhist monastery, wrote the first book about tea entitled, *Ch'a Ching*. His theories on tea, which he developed in relation to the doctrine of harmony, resulted in a tea culture in China that characterized tea drinking as a symbolic meditation.

Certainly, proselytizing by Buddhist monks in Asia, who wandered from monastery to monastery, was key in promoting wide spread tea consumption. It was centuries, however, before tea was finally known throughout the world.

A Long Journey to Europe
and Overseas

In 1285, Marco Polo traveled the famous Silk Road and returned to Venice with stories about tea. But it was Vasco da Gama who brought back actual Indian tea in 1498. In 1637, tea finally experienced a real breakthrough with the establishment by the Dutch of the Dutch East Indian Company, which imported tea from China and Japan. The English followed suit in 1650 when they founded the English East Indian Company. Thus, tea finally arrived in Europe. At first it was available only to nobility, but in subsequent years, England experienced a tea frenzy. Due to the large volume of trade transacted at an advantageous moment in the market, tea began to find its way into the cups of the middle-class. Royalists and admirers of the English court were soon imitating the king's wife. The Portuguese Princess, Catherine of Braganza officially introduced tea time in the court due to the high rate of alcohol consumption. Europe's entire aristocracy followed this example. During this same time, major porcelain manufacturers were coming into being and creating the appropriately opulent tea time accoutrements.

It was also in 1650 that the Dutch governor in America, Peter Stuyvesant, ordered tea to be sent to his fellow countrymen who had immigrated to New Amsterdam (now New York).

In Russia, the tea trade between the Tsar Alexis and the Chinese Ambassador to Moscow began flourishing even earlier. In 1618, the Tsar received a gift of tea, after which a lively tea trade developed in the country.

Tea—A Very Special Herb

The original Chinese name "Chi" means "life energy," a word origin that seems likely enough. A relationship to this name can be detected in many other languages: For example, "Ch'a" in present-day China, "Cha" in Japan, "Caj" in Russia, "Cay" in Turkey, "Chai" in India, "Tee" in German-speaking countries and, finally, "Tea" in Britain and other English speaking countries.

From a purely botanical point of view, the tea plant is a member of the camellia family. Scientists differentiate between two "original" varieties of tea: The Chinese plant (Thea or Camellia sinensis), and the Assam plant (Thea or Camellia assamica). They have not been able to determine which of the two is older. Extensive cross-breeding has resulted in Assam hybrids that are now the basis for most tea plantings in the world.

Cultivation

The two original varieties of the evergreen tea plant grow very differently. Even without pruning, the Chinese plant remains shrub-like and reaches a maximum height of 10–13 feet. The Assamica plant, on the other hand, can grow up to 50 feet. Cultivated in plantations, both types of plant are pruned for practical and economic reasons so that they grow as many branches as possible and do not exceed a height of about five feet.

The tea plant is very demanding. Under favorable environmental conditions—such as moderate temperatures (rare and moderate frost), lots of sun, lots of precipitation evenly distributed throughout the year, and fertile, permeable or well-drained acid soil—is guaranteed to produce a good harvest. The tea plant thrives under these conditions even at altitudes above 6800 feet. Although the yield decreases as the altitude increases and the bushes are smaller, the absolute best teas come from high-altitude regions such as Assam and Darjeeling in India.

The primary tea cultivating countries are Bangladesh, China, India, Iran, Japan, Java, Malaysia, New Guinea, Singapore, Sri Lanka, Sumatra, Taiwan, Tibet and Vietnam. India and Sri Lanka are the world's largest tea exporters. Green and black teas mainly originate in the Far East. Other countries that cultivate tea in Africa, Europe and South America export Rooibus, fruit, mate and lapacho tea, as well as various types of herb tea.

On traditional, high-quality plantations, all tea is harvested by hand, using a method of plucking two leaves and a bud. This method ensures the highest quality while also preparing the plant for the next harvest. Tea plantations that use mechanical picking equipment produce a much lower quality standard.

The harvest time depends on the particular region of cultivation. In Assam, India, which is the world's largest continuous highland region of tea cultivation, only one harvest ("flush") is performed from the end of May to mid-July. In southern India, there is one harvest between December and March. In the famous Indian tea region of Darjeeling, there are two main harvesting seasons per year that are very different from one another. The first harvest, from the end of February to early April, is called the "first flush" and is when the tea with the finest aroma is collected. The second harvest ("second flush") is from the end of May to the end of July and produces heavier, spicier tea. As the milder of the two, second flush tea has many fans. Other intermediate harvests in this region yield lower-quality tea. Tea growing regions such as Sri Lanka permit harvesting all year round.

Production Methods for
Black and Green Tea

Black and green teas are comprised of leaves from the same harvests; they differ only with regard to their processing. Immediately after the harvest, leaves intended for black tea are "wilted," e.g. they are spread on drying racks to extract about 30 percent of their moisture, making them soft and pliable for further processing. The tea leaves are then put through a roller, where rotating cylinders break up the cells, causing a chemical reaction between the cell sap and oxygen which causes the release of essential oils. After being sieved, the tea leaves undergo a fermentation or oxidation process that is several hours long. During this procedure, the yellow-green leaves are spread on tables and exposed to temperatures of 90–105°F and high humidity, gradually turning the leaves a copper color.

Tea leaves intended for green tea are not fermented but are simply roasted (in China) or steamed (in Japan) and then dried. This is why the leaves retain their olive-green color.

Both fermented and unfermented tea leaves are then conveyed through a hot-air dryer at about 175°F so they can be stored without spoiling. This procedure is also responsible for giving black tea its final color.

When traditional processing methods are used, the tea leaves are sorted by hand and sieved into different leaf grades. A distinction is made between "leaf tea," which contains almost no broken pieces, and "broken tea," which is reduced to different sizes.

When a mechanical process is used, the tea leaves are processed through a cutter, which reduces them to different grades, depending on their intended use. (See the glossary on pages 74–79 for an explanation of the terms "leaf tea," "broken," "cutter," "dust" and "fannings.")

Finally, the most important phase of tea processing occurs–the tasting. "Tea tasters" classify the raw products according to color, strength and aroma. They decide on the ratio of teas in the blends, thereby determining the quality of the final product. Based on the information supplied by the tasters, the teas are purchased and packaged in the country where they were produced and imported to the consuming countries.

Green Tea—A Philosophy

Because fresh tea leaves are "only" steamed or roasted gently and then dried, green tea can be considered a nutritious, natural product.

Green tea is a shining star in the nutrition and wellness sector, mainly because of the astonishing properties attributed to it. Compared to black tea, it contains higher concentrations of healthy ingredients such as important trace elements, a multitude of vitamins, antioxidants and bioactive substances. In order to take full advantage of the health benefits of green tea, you would have to drink at least eight cups a day over a period of years. Nevertheless, drinking green tea is a philosophical position and a way of life.

Japan is its leading producer and produces only green tea. The most important Japanese varieties are Sencha, Gyokuro, Mattcha, Bancha and Honjicha.

Black Tea—A Science

In many countries, drinking black tea is considered a science. Should infusion be short or long? What type of water, what type of tea and what amount should be used? Do you drink it plain or flavored? What cups do you serve it in? Do you serve it with white sugar, brown sugar or rock sugar; with milk or cream? With a shot of lemon juice, lime juice or alcohol? Even the cookies served with black tea can become a sort of pledge of allegiance. Discussions that arise can be similar to those around wine: What type of soil? What leaf grade and what harvest?

Specialty shops can offer helpful advice, both to passionate tea drinkers and to tea amateurs. Eventually, however, everyone learns to regard Second Flush Darjeeling as the Champagne of tea.

The Right Way to Prepare Tea

There are several factors to be considered when selecting a teapot and preparing tea:

1. Use a flavor-neutral material such as china, stoneware, clay, stainless steel or glass. Avoid cheap pots that are metal or ceramic with questionable glazes.

2. Select a teapot with the "belly of a Buddha" so that the tea leaves have room to expand after you add the water.

3. Use the designated pot only for tea and not for anything else. After continuous tea preparation, a film will form on the inside of the pot. Do not remove this film with a coarse scouring pad or detergent. It contributes to the fine aroma and flavor.

4. Use different teapots for different types of tea—for example, one for green and plain black teas, one for herb teas and one for strongly flavored teas.

5. Before using, rinse out the pot with hot water.

6. Tea tastes best made with soft, non-chlorinated water. Water that is too hard forms a cloudy film on the surface and spoils the aroma. If that's the type of water you have, use bottled or filtered water. Otherwise, briefly bring fresh tap water to a rolling boil and pour immediately onto the tea.

7. Do not use a tea ball. It inhibits the development of the aroma of delicate tea varieties. Instead, select flavor-neutral paper filters or suitable tea nets.

8. While black tea is steeping, the following rule of thumb applies: A small amount of tea steeped for up to five minutes has a calming effect; a large amount of tea steeped for less than three minutes has a stimulating effect.

9. Green tea is not prepared with boiling water, but with water heated to about 175°F. For this purpose, let freshly boiled water stand for 5–8 minutes before pouring it into a pot containing about 1 level tablespoon of tea. Steep for 3–5 minutes. You can steep the same leaves three times; the second infusion is considered to be the best.

10. If you use loose tea (without a paper filter or tea net), transfer the finished tea to a serving pot that has first been rinsed out with hot water.

Teas & Punches—
Hot and Stimulating

East-Frisian-Style Tea

4 cups boiling water,
2 tablespoons black tea leaves (East Frisian blend),
Sugar cubes (as desired), Cream (as desired)

Pour half the boiling water over the tea leaves and steep for about 5 minutes. Add remaining water. Transfer tea to a serving pot.

Place 2 sugar cubes in each cup. Pour tea into cup. Carefully place a small teaspoonful of cream on top to form a cloud. Do not stir!

🍃 Serve with East Frisian cookies. If desired, drizzle a little rum over the sugar.

Scottish-Style Tea

$1/2$ cup whisky (or more if desired),
$1/2$ cup sugar, 2 cups strong, hot black tea,
$1/2$ cup whipped cream, Freshly grated nutmeg

Pour whisky in 4 heavy cups and stir in sugar. Add tea and cover each serving with a heavy layer of whipped cream. Grate a little nutmeg on top.

British Tea for Two

The well-known book *Asterix in Britain* could not go without mentioning "tea time." Every afternoon at precisely 5 o'clock, the island's inhabitants drank "hot water with a spot of milk." Asterix then brewed a sort of substitute magic potion using herbs from the druid Getafix to fortify the British in their fight against the Romans. Following their joint victory, the Brits "Mcanix" and "O'Veroptimistix" want only these herbs for their hot water. When Asterix asks Getafix what herbs he gave him, the druid answers, "Oh, they're a plant that comes from far-off barbaric lands...called tea."

Preheat the pot. Add 1 level teaspoon of tea per cup to the pot and immediately pour in boiling water. In each cup, pour a little cold milk and stir in a little sugar. Steep tea for no more than 4–5 minutes in the pot, then pour into the cups.

Russian Tea

Although Vodka is Russia's national drink, tea occupies first place as the Russian's favorite nonalcoholic beverage. It's very appropriate in a country where winter temperatures can drop as low as 12°F, as they do in many parts of Russia. Russians have been serving tea in samovars (meaning "self-boil") since the 17th century. This charming contraption is manufactured in Tula, a small town south of Moscow and comes in various sizes and materials, including copper, brass and silver. Originally, a charcoal fire in the central tube heated samovars, but today they are mainly electric.

Rinse a china teapot ("chainik" in Russian) with hot water. Prepare a strong black tea in the pot, steep for 3–5 minutes, then set on top of the samovar. Pour tea into glasses or cups and mix with boiling water from the samovar at a ratio of one to four.

For an authentic tea experience, hold a cube of sugar between your front teeth and let the tea flow through it as you drink.

🍃 In Russia, tea is traditionally served with "warenje," preserved fruits sweetened with sugar, but can also be accompanied by cake or pierogi.

Austrian Jagertee (Hunter's Tea)

Jagertee is a winter beverage intended as a warmer-upper after skiing. Consequently, it contains a considerable amount of alcohol. The most popular version comprises black tea with a shot of rum. A combination of black tea, rum and fruit brandy is also a favorite. The following recipe uses wine.

> 2 cups freshly brewed black tea,
> 2 cups red wine, 1 cinnamon stick,
> 2 whole cloves, 2 teaspoons sugar,
> ½ cup rum and/or ½ cup fruit brandy

In a saucepan, heat black tea, wine, cinnamon, cloves and sugar for about 5 minutes without boiling. Pour into glasses or cups and add rum and/or fruit brandy.

Wind Force 9 to 12

The "9 to 12" scale refers to the alcohol content. The stronger the wind blows, the higher the waves and the nicer it is to stay home and drink spiked, hot tea.

> 12 sugar cubes, 2 lemons,
> 2 cups hot black tea, ½ cup port wine,
> ½ cup red wine, 3 tablespoons brandy

Rub sugar cubes onto the lemon peel until they've soaked up the citrus flavor. In a small saucepan, dissolve sugar in black tea. Add port, red wine and brandy. Heat briefly without boiling. Pour into 4 tea glasses and check whether the strength of the drink corresponds to the wind force outdoors...

Turkish Tea

3 tablespoons Turkish black tea leaves,
Sugar (as desired)

Place 2 stacking teapots on the stove, one on top of the other. Fill the bottom teapot (which must be heat-resistant) with water. In the top pot (preferably china), place 2 teaspoons black tea per cup. As soon as the water in the bottom pot boils, pour half of it into the china pot and let steep for about 10 minutes.

To serve, fill glasses half full of tea and top up with boiling water. Add sugar as desired.

🍃 You'll find special glasses and two-tier teapots in well-stocked Turkish shops. You can also prepare this tea with a simple tea kettle and teapot. In this case, set the teapot on a tea warmer to keep the tea concentrate hot.

Ginger Tea with Lime

½ inch fresh ginger root,
2 tablespoons black tea leaves,
4 cups boiling water, 1 lime, Sugar cubes

Peel ginger, dice finely and combine with tea leaves. Add boiling water and steep for 4–5 minutes. In the meantime, peel lime, slice thinly and place 1 slice in each cup. Add a sugar cube on top of the lime and pour tea.

Middle-Eastern Spiced Tea with Fruit

1 apple, 4 cups prepared black tea,
Juice from 2 oranges, 2 cups pineapple juice,
⅓ cup sugar, ½ cinnamon stick,
1 pinch ground allspice, 6 coriander seeds,
2 whole cloves
Plus: ½ cup cream, Cinnamon

Peel apple, cut into quarters, remove core and dice finely. In a saucepan, heat remaining ingredients and steep for 10 minutes. Pour tea through a strainer into glasses or cups. Whip cream, spoon onto tea and dust with cinnamon.

Moroccan Tea

In Arab countries, the people consume enormous amounts of coffee (kahwa) and tea. Whereas coffee is very expensive, tea is economical. The men meet in special tea houses to enjoy a glass with their circle of friends. Women, on the other hand, have to drink their tea at home.

½ cup black tea leaves,
Lots of sugar (as desired), Cardamom,
Anise or jasmine (as desired),
½ bunch fresh mint

Brew a strong tea, sweeten with lots of sugar and stir in spices as desired. Just before serving, add mint leaves.

🌿 In many Arab countries, tea is traditionally drunk from glasses without handles. It is served after meals with mixed fruits and sunflower seeds.

My Tea Pharisee

The following story has been immortalized in the Rum Museum in Flensburg, Germany.

In 1827, Pastor Gustav Bleyer tried to save his village "flock" from destruction through overindulgence in alcohol. He forbid people from drinking in his presence. One day, at the baptismal celebration of Farmer Johannsen, the pastor stayed on too long. In order to get around him, the guest's simply poured rum into their sweetened coffee, topped it with a pretty large dollop of whipped cream and happily sipped their new creation. Eventually, the pastor was mistakenly served this beverage. He scolded those present by calling them, "You Pharisees!" and thus christened the hot satanic beverage as well. So, you might ask, what does that have to do with tea? I make the same drink and substitute tea for coffee because I enjoy repeating this story.

> 4 cups fresh-made black tea,
> Sugar and rum (as desired),
> Whipped cream, Powdered sugar,
> Grated peel from 1 lemon (optional)

Stir sugar and rum into the prepared tea and top with a thick dollop of whipped cream. If desired, garnish with powdered sugar and grated lemon peel.

Flaming Punch with Black Tea

British sailors brought punch to Europe in the early 17th century. The name is derived from the Sanskrit word "panca," meaning "five." A punch comprises five basic ingredients: Rum or wine, lemon juice, sugar, spices, tea, water or milk.

Although the original recipe doesn't call for tea, this version tastes fantastic. Tea takes the place of half the red wine.

4 cups briefly brewed black tea,
4 cups dry red wine, Juice from 1 lemon,
5 whole cloves, 2 oranges, Sugar (as desired),
2 cups rum (54 percent vol. alcohol)

In a saucepan, combine tea, wine, lemon juice and cloves. Heat slowly. In the meantime, rinse oranges and remove peel in spirals, leaving behind the white membrane. Squeeze juice. Add peel and juice to the saucepan. Add sugar and rum to the saucepan, continue heating for 1–2 minutes and serve.

Iced Teas & Mixed Drinks— Cool and Refreshing

Cold Tea Grog

In its original form, the famous tea beverage "grog" was served cold. It was named after Admiral Vernon, known to sailors as "Old Grogram." According to the story, sailors were given a generous allowance of rum to boost their morale during long voyages. Old Grogram decided to stretch his supply of rum by watering it down, while also adding lemon juice and sugar to prevent the dreaded disease scurvy.

4 cups cooled black tea,
Sugar cubes and rum (as desired),
4 lemon quarters

Pour tea into cups or special grog glasses. Stir in sugar cubes and rum. Serve each glass with 1 lemon quarter.

🍃 Although grog was originally prepared "only" with water, this version has much more flavor. And, as it is said in northern Germany, rum is mandatory, sugar is optional and water is unnecessary!

East Frisian Iced Tea

$\frac{1}{2}$ cup cream, 3 tablespoons powdered sugar,
2 cups cold black tea, About 3 tablespoons sugar,
16 ice cubes, 3 tablespoons brandy

Whip cream with powdered sugar until stiff. Sweeten tea with sugar and pour into 4 glasses with 4 ice cubes each. Drizzle with brandy and garnish with a thick layer of whipped cream.

🌿 Always serve alcoholic tea beverages with cookies or snacks to mitigate the effects of the alcohol.

Vitamin Kick with Sea Buckthorn

1 cup sea buckthorn juice (available at most
health food stores), 1 cup cold black tea,
Juice from $\frac{1}{2}$ lemon,
1 cup cherry juice, 12 ice cubes,
4 toothpicks and fresh cherries (optional)

Combine sea buckthorn juice, tea, lemon juice and cherry juice. Place 3 ice cubes in tall glasses and add juice mixture. If desired, thread 1 cherry onto each toothpick and place in each glass as a garnish.

Cold Krambambuli

3½ tablespoons black tea leaves,
4 cups boiling water, 2 bottles white wine,
2 cups sugar, Grated peel from 1 lemon,
1 cup rum

Combine tea leaves and boiling water. Steep for 5 minutes. Strain tea and let cool. In a punch bowl, mix wine, sugar, lemon peel and rum. Add cold tea. Sweeten to taste and serve.

🍃 You can also serve Krambambuli hot.

Tea Cocktail with Fruit

1 small orange, 1 banana,
$1/3$ cup pineapple chunks (canned),
2 cups cold black tea, 3 tablespoons sugar,
$1/2$ cup mixed flavor fruit juice,
4 long cocktail skewers

Peel orange, removing the white membrane and cut into bite-sized pieces. Peel banana and slice. Alternately thread orange, banana and pineapple pieces onto 4 long cocktail skewers. Combine black tea, sugar and fruit juice and pour into 4 glasses. Place a fruit skewer in each glass.

🌿 Serve this cocktail with ice cubes to make it very refreshing.

Limoncello on Iced Tea

Limoncello is a lemon liqueur made exclusively from lemons from around Sorrento and the Amalfi Coast in Italy. These lemons have a perfect balance of sweet and sour flavors. Be sure to try it on the rocks, drizzled on vanilla ice cream or, in tea as described below.

2 cups cold black tea, 3 tablespoons sugar,
12 ice cubes, $1/2$ cup Limoncello

Combine black tea and sugar. Place ice cubes in 4 tall glasses, drizzle with 1 tablespoon Limoncello and add tea. Serve with long spoons or swizzle sticks.

Cold and Hot

About 20 fresh lemon balm leaves,
1 cup Prosecco, 2 cups hot green tea,
4 lime slices

Rinse lemon balm leaves and place one leaf in each compartment of an ice cube tray. Carefully add Prosecco. Place tray in the freezer for at least 4 hours.

Place 5 lemon balm ice cubes in each of 4 highball glasses and add green tea. Cut a slit in the lime slices and place them on the rims of the glasses.

🍃 If possible, prepare at the table: Lemon balm leaves in Prosecco ice cubes look so spectacular. Your guests will surely admire them!

Cakes & Pastries—
Made or Served with Tea

Punch Cake with Black Tea

Makes 1 bundt pan

For the batter: ¹/₂ cup softened butter,
¹/₂ cup sugar, 3 eggs, 1 pinch salt,
Grated peel from 1 lemon,
¹/₃ cup ground almonds, 1¹/₂ cups flour,
3 teaspoons baking powder,
¹/₃ cup cold black tea, ¹/₃ cup orange juice
For the glaze: ¹/₃ cup powdered sugar,
Juice from 1 lemon
Plus: Butter and flour for the pan

For the batter: In a bowl, beat butter and sugar until fluffy. Stir in eggs, salt and grated lemon peel. Gradually mix in almonds, flour and baking powder. Stir in black tea and orange juice.

Preheat oven to 400°F. Butter and a flour bundt pan. Spoon batter into the pan and bake in the oven for about 1 hour until golden. Remove from the oven, let cool, then carefully reverse onto a plate.

For the glaze: Mix powdered sugar and lemon juice until smooth and spread on top of the cake.

English Tea Bread

Makes 1 loaf pan

1½ cups flour, 1 packet dry yeast,
3 tablespoons sugar, 1 teaspoon,
⅓ cup condensed milk, 1 egg, 1 pinch salt,
1 teaspoon freshly chopped ginger,
2 tablespoons raisins, 1 tablespoon whiskey,
Butter and flour for the pan

Sift flour into a bowl and make a well in the center. Place yeast, sugar, vanilla and condensed milk in the well. Dust with flour from the edges and let stand for 15 minutes.

Add ⅔ cup water, egg, salt, ginger, raisins and whiskey and process into a pliable dough. Cover and let rise in a warm place for 30 minutes.

Preheat oven to 400°F. Butter and flour a loaf pan, spoon in dough and smooth out the surface. Bake in the oven for up to 50 minutes until golden.

🍃 This bread can also be made in a bread maker.

Lemon Cake

It's said that tea without lemon is like coffee without milk. The following recipe is for a cake containing so much lemon that the tea won't need any. Another way to bring the flavors together is to dip the cake into the tea.

Makes 1 bundt pan

1 cup softened butter, 1 cup sugar,
4 large eggs, 1 cup flour,
3 teaspoons baking powder,
Juice and grated peel from 1 lemon,
$^2/_3$ cup finely diced candied lemon peel
Plus: Butter and flour for the pan,
Powdered sugar for garnish

In a bowl, beat butter, sugar and eggs until creamy. Gradually stir in flour, baking powder, lemon juice, lemon peel and candied lemon peel.

Preheat oven to 400°F. Butter and flour a bundt pan. Add batter and smooth out the surface. Bake in the oven for up to 1 hour until golden-brown. Let cool briefly in the pan, then reverse onto a plate. Dust with a thick layer of powdered sugar.

🌿 You can also top the cake with a glaze of lemon juice and powdered sugar.

Rum Poppy Seed Cake

Makes 1 bundt pan

4 medium eggs, $\frac{1}{3}$ cup sugar,
$\frac{1}{3}$ cup softened butter, 3 tablespoons rum,
3 tablespoons flour, 3 tablespoons breadcrumbs,
$\frac{1}{2}$ cup ground poppy seeds
Plus: Butter and flour for the pan,
Powdered sugar for garnish

Separate eggs. Beat 3 tablespoons of sugar and butter until fluffy. Gradually stir in rum, flour, breadcrumbs and poppy seeds. Beat egg whites with remaining sugar until creamy but not stiff and fold in.

Preheat oven to 350°F. Butter and flour the pan. Add batter and smooth out the surface. Bake in the oven for about 45 minutes. Remove, let cool in the pan for 5 minutes, then reverse onto a plate. Dust with powdered sugar and serve warm.

Walnut Cookies with Green Tea

1 cup ground walnuts,
1 1/2 cups powdered sugar, 1/3 cup cold green tea
For the glaze: Juice from 1 lemon,
1/3 cup powdered sugar
Plus: Powdered sugar for the work surface,
Walnut halves for garnish

On a countertop, knead together ground walnuts, powdered sugar and green tea to form a smooth dough. Dust the work surface with powdered sugar and carefully roll out dough to a thickness of about 1/2 inch. Using a cookie cutter or a glass, cut out cookies and place on a baking sheet lined with parchment paper. Cover cookies with another sheet of parchment paper and let dry for at least 8 hours (preferably overnight).

For the glaze: Mix lemon juice and powdered sugar until smooth and spread onto cookies. Garnish each cookie with 1 walnut half.

Instead of walnuts, you can also use hazelnuts.

🌿 Since there's no baking required, these hearty cookies can be made anywhere.

Scones

Tea time would be incomplete without English scones. At a traditional English "cream tea," they're served with butter, clotted cream and strawberry jam.

1 cup flour, 3 teaspoons baking powder,
1 tablespoon sour cream,
1 tablespoon softened butter,
1 tablespoon sugar, 1 pinch salt,
Up to ½ cup warm milk,
1 tablespoon melted butter

Preheat oven to 400°F. Sift flour and baking powder onto a work surface and make a well in the center. Fill the well with sour cream, butter, sugar and salt. Carefully add milk and knead all ingredients together to form a soft dough.

Shape dough into a cylinder with a diameter of about ½ inch and cut into slices about ½ inch thick. Place slices on a baking sheet lined with parchment paper and bake in the oven for about 10 minutes, until golden. Remove and brush the surfaces with melted butter.

Shortbread

These Scottish cookies are a classic among tea pastries. They're worth every calorie!

1 cup flour, ²/₃ cup sugar, 1 pinch salt,
¹/₂ cup cornstarch, 1¹/₂ cups cold butter

Preheat oven to 350°F. Sift flour onto a work surface. Distribute sugar, salt, cornstarch and butter cut into pieces onto the work surface. Quickly knead together into a smooth dough. Roll out evenly onto a baking sheet and pierce at regular intervals with a fork. Bake in the oven for 35–45 minutes until golden. Cut into bite-sized rectangles.

Madeleines

This delicious pastry, dunked in lime-blossom tea, brought back a whole world of memories for the hero of Marcel Proust's famous epic, *Remembrance of Things Past*. Madelines also taste great with green or black tea.

6 medium eggs, $1/2$ cup sugar,
Pulp from 1 vanilla bean,
Grated peel from $1/2$ lemon, $1/2$ packet dry yeast,
$1/2$ cup flour, $1/2$ cup melted butter,
Butter for the pan

Beat eggs and sugar until foamy. Stir in vanilla pulp and lemon peel. Combine yeast and flour. Carefully work into egg mixture with a wooden spoon. Stir in melted butter. Cover batter and let stand in a cool place for 1 hour.

Preheat oven to 400°F. Butter a madeleine pan then spoon in batter. Bake in the oven for about 10 minutes until golden (test with a toothpick!).

🍃 If you don't have a madeleine pan, use a buttered muffin pan.

Brioches

1½ cups flour, 3 tablespoons sugar,
3 tablespoons yeast, ⅓ cup lukewarm water,
⅓ cup softened butter, 3 medium egg yolks,
Grated peel from ½ lemon, ½ cup cream
Plus: Flour for the work surface,
2 medium egg yolks for brushing on

Sift flour into a bowl and form a well in the center. Sprinkle in sugar. Stir in yeast and water. Cover and let stand for about 15 minutes. Process with remaining ingredients into a pliable dough, cover and let rise in a warm place for 30 minutes.

On a floured work surface, knead dough thoroughly and divide into about 20 portions. Remove a small piece of dough from each portion and roll into a little ball. Shape larger portions into balls and press the small ball onto the top of each.

Preheat oven to 400°F. Place brioches on a baking sheet lined with parchment paper, leaving adequate spacing in between. Whisk together egg yolks and 2 tablespoons water, then brush onto brioches. Bake in the oven for up to 30 minutes until golden.

🍃 Eating fresh brioches with tea or dipping them in tea is a heavenly experience.

Chocolate Muffins with Cinnamon

Makes 12 muffins

> 7 ounces milk chocolate, $^2/_3$ cup milk,
> 1 cup flour, 3 teaspoons baking powder,
> $^2/_3$ cup softened butter, $^1/_2$ cup sugar,
> 2 teaspoons vanilla, 1 medium egg,
> $^1/_2$ teaspoon cinnamon,
> Butter and sugar for the pan

Break chocolate into pieces and melt in a heat-resistant bowl over a hot double boiler. Stir in milk. In a second bowl, sift flour and baking powder.

In a wide bowl, beat butter, sugar, vanilla and egg until creamy. Add chocolate milk, then mix in flour.

Preheat oven to 400°F. Butter muffin pan and coat with sugar. Add batter and smooth out the surface.

Bake in the oven for about 20 minutes until golden. Remove, let cool in the pan for 5 minutes and remove carefully.

Plum Canapés

1 cup flour, 3 tablespoons yeast,
$^1/_3$ cup sugar, $^1/_2$ cup lukewarm milk,
$^1/_3$ cup softened butter cut into pieces,
1 small egg, Salt, $4^1/_2$ pounds plums,
3 tablespoons pearl sugar,
Cinnamon (optional),
Butter and flour for the baking sheet

Sift flour into a bowl, form a well in the center and sprinkle in yeast. Sprinkle sugar and add milk. Cover and let stand for 15 minutes.

Add butter, egg and 1 pinch salt and knead into a pliable dough. Cover and let rise in a warm place for 30 minutes.

In the meantime, rinse plums, remove pits and cut into quarters. Butter and flour a baking sheet.

Preheat oven to 400°F. Roll out dough and transfer to the baking sheet. Top with plums evenly spaced. Combine pearl sugar and cinnamon and sprinkle on top.

Bake in the oven for 35–40 minutes until golden. Remove, let cool briefly and cut into narrow canapés.

🍃 With this pastry, black tea tastes better than green tea. If desired, serve with whipped cream.

Philippine Rice Cake

To aid digestion, serve this delicacy with black tea and lemon.

1 cup long-grain rice, Salt, 2 medium eggs,
$1/2$ cup sugar, 2 teaspoons vanilla,
$1/2$ teaspoon grated nutmeg, $1/3$ cup flour,
1 packet baking powder, 4 cups vegetable oil,
Powdered sugar

Cook rice in boiling salted water according to package directions. Let cool.

Beat eggs, sugar, vanilla and nutmeg until frothy. Fold in rice, flour and baking powder. Process until dough is sticky.

In a wide, tall, pan or pot, heat vegetable oil. Using 2 tablespoons and each time rinsing the spoons in cold water, transfer mounds of dough to the hot oil and deep-fry on all sides for 3–5 minutes until golden and crispy. Remove from oil, drain briefly on paper towels and arrange on a platter. Dust with a thick coating of powdered sugar and serve warm with a pot of black tea.

🍃 A nice addition to the traditional European afternoon tea time.

Hearty Sour Cream Rolls

3½ ounces bacon, thinly sliced,
1 small onion, 1 teaspoon butter,
2 cups flour, 3 teaspoons baking powder,
1 teaspoon salt, 3 tablespoons honey,
1 cup low fat sour cream, 2 medium eggs
Plus: Flour for the work surface, 1 egg yolk

Finely dice bacon. Peel onion and chop finely. In a hot pan, render bacon. Stir in onion and butter and sweat until translucent. Remove from heat.

In a bowl and using an electric mixer with a dough-hook attachment, gradually process flour, baking powder, salt, honey, sour cream, eggs and pan contents into a smooth dough.

Knead dough thoroughly on a floured work surface. Divide into 12 pieces and shape into round rolls. Using a moistened knife blade, cut an X into the surface of each roll and brush with whisked egg yolk.

Preheat oven to 400°F. Transfer rolls to a baking sheet lined with parchment paper, leaving adequate spacing in between. Bake in the oven for about 30 minutes until golden.

🍃 Enjoy as a second breakfast at 9:30 am or with 5 o'clock tea—and only with butter. These rolls taste best with black tea.

Jellies & Desserts—
Sweet and Fruity

Apple Jelly with Green Tea

4 stalks fresh peppermint, 3 cups apple juice,
1 cup hard cider, 1 cup green tea,
1 pouch liquid fruit pectin, 2 whole cloves

Rinse mint, pat dry, remove leaves from stems and cut into fine strips. Combine apple juice, cider, green tea, liquid fruit pectin and cloves and bring to a boil while stirring. Boil uncovered for 3 minutes, then remove from heat and stir in mint.

Transfer immediately to hot, sterilized jelly jars and seal tightly.

 Instead of mint, fold chopped green tea leaves into the jelly.

Cherry-Vanilla Jam with Black Tea

All tea lovers will love this jam—but so will many others!

2½ pounds cherries, 2 vanilla beans,
1 cup weak black tea, Juice from ½ lemon,
1 pouch liquid fruit pectin

Rinse cherries and remove pits. Cut 1 cup cherries in half and set aside. Purée remaining cherries in a blender. Slit open vanilla beans lengthwise and scrape out pulp.

In a saucepan, combine puréed cherries, vanilla pulp, cherry halves, black tea, lemon juice and liquid fruit pectin. Bring to a boil while stirring constantly. Simmer uncovered over medium heat for 4 minutes while stirring constantly. Transfer immediately to hot, sterilized jelly jars and seal tight

Green Tea Jelly with Lime Wedges

2 limes, 2 cups green tea,
1/2 packet liquid fruit pectin

Rinse limes and dry thoroughly. Using a sharp knife, remove peel in spirals, leaving behind the white membrane. Cut lime peel spirals into narrower, smaller pieces. Remove white membrane from limes and cut flesh into small, uniform pieces.

In a saucepan, combine tea and liquid fruit pectin and bring to a boil. Add lime pieces and peels. Simmer uncovered for 3–4 minutes while stirring constantly. Transfer immediately to hot, sterilized jelly jars and seal tightly.

🍃 Green Tea Jelly is ideal for an English breakfast.

Orange Tea Jelly

1 orange, 2 cups black tea, 3 cups orange juice,
1 packet liquid fruit pectin, 4 whole cloves

Rinse orange, dry thoroughly and use a zester to remove the finest possible zest. Squeeze juice. In a saucepan, combine black tea, orange juice, fruit pectin and cloves. Bring to a boil. Stir in orange zest and simmer uncovered for 3–4 minutes. Transfer immediately to hot, sterilized jelly jars and seal tightly.

🍃 If desired, add the zest from 1 lemon too.

Green Tea Coconut Mousse
Served in a Pineapple

2 baby pineapples,
½ cup canned coconut milk, ½ cup green tea,
3 egg whites, ⅓ cup powdered sugar,
½ cup grated coconut for garnish

Cut baby pineapples in half lengthwise and hollow out the halves. Measure ½ cup of pineapple and purée in a blender with coconut milk and green tea. Place purée in the freezer for about 20 minutes. Chop remaining pineapple into small pieces.

Beat egg whites with powdered sugar until stiff and fold into partially frozen purée. Spoon into pineapple halves and garnish with pineapple pieces and grated coconut.

🍃 To be served, of course, with green tea.

Stir-Fried Fruit Rice

3 tablespoons sesame seeds,
1 small mango, 1 baby pineapple,
2 tablespoons butter, 2 tablespoons sugar,
$1/2$ cup cooked glutinous rice,
$1/3$ cup canned coconut milk

Heat wok and stir-fry sesame seeds until they give off a fragrance, then remove.

Peel mango and baby pineapple. Cut fruit into small pieces. Heat wok and melt butter and sugar while stirring.

Add fruit pieces, toss several times and then fold in rice. Add coconut milk and mix carefully. Transfer to 4 soup bowls and garnish with sesame seeds. Serve with green tea.

🍃 If desired, top fruit rice with several scoops of ice cream and drizzle with green tea.

Blue-Green Tea Sorbet

1 lime, ½ cup Blue Curaçao, 3 tablespoons
lime syrup, 2 large egg whites, 1 small pinch salt,
½ cup cold green tea, About 12 lemon balm leaves,
Juice from ½ lemon, Powdered sugar,
1 cup lukewarm green tea

Rinse lime, dry and use a zester to remove the finest possible zest. Combine zest, Blue Curaçao and lime syrup. Mix thoroughly.

Beat egg whites with salt until very stiff. Stir in green tea one teaspoonful at a time. Fold egg whites into the lime mixture. Transfer to an ice cream maker that is already running and freeze for about 40 minutes.

In the meantime, rinse lemon balm leaves, dip in lemon juice and dredge individually in powdered sugar. Arrange on a plate, leaving adequate spacing in between and place in the freezer for 15 minutes.

To serve, scoop sorbet into martini glasses, drizzle lukewarm green tea around the edges and garnish with frozen, sugared leaves.

🌿 Ideal as a refreshing intermediate course in a fancy meal.

🌿 If you don't have an ice cream maker, place the mixture in the freezer for 3–4 hours, stirring hourly.

Tea Zabaglione on Mango Salad

2 ripe mangos, 2 tablespoons rum,
5 medium egg yolks, 1/2 cup sugar,
1/2 cup weak black tea,
2 tablespoons sliced almonds for garnish

Peel mangos and cut flesh into uniform pieces.
Arrange in 4 soup bowls and drizzle with 1 tablespoon
of rum.

Beat egg yolks with sugar in a heat-resistant bowl
until creamy and place over a hot double boiler. Beat
into an airy cream, gradually stirring in black tea and
remaining rum. Remove bowl from double boiler, beat
cream briefly once again and scoop onto mango salad.
Garnish with sliced almonds.

If desired, vary with bananas, oranges, grapes or a
mixture of fruit.

Frozen Green Tea Yogurt
with Cucumbers

1 cucumber, 3 tablespoons cold green tea with lemon,
$^1/_3$ cup sugar, 3 medium egg whites, Salt,
1 cup whole milk yogurt, 1 tablespoon honey,
$^1/_3$ cup lukewarm green tea

Peel cucumber, cut in half lengthwise and remove seeds. Grate one half finely. Cover the other half and set aside. Combine grated cucumber, cold green tea and sugar. Cover and refrigerate for 1 hour.

Place cucumber mixture in a strainer. Press out liquid with a spoon and save. Discard strainer contents.

Using an electric mixer, beat egg whites with 1 pinch salt until stiff. Slowly beat in cucumber-tea liquid. Combine egg-white mixture and yogurt and transfer to a bowl. Place in the freezer for at least 6 hours, stirring mixture several times an hour.

Finely dice the cucumber half that was set aside. Thoroughly mix honey, green tea and diced cucumber. Scoop into 4 dessert glasses. Before serving frozen yogurt, let thaw for 5 minutes. Scoop yogurt onto the diced cucumber in the glasses.

🌿 Garnish with chopped dill or lemon balm leaves.

🌿 Serve this "fruit-and-vegetable" frozen yogurt as an intermediate course in a fancy meal. It's refreshing and prepares diners for the culinary delights to come.

Tiramisu with Green Tea

Makes 4 teacups

1 lemon, 1 large egg yolk, 3 tablespoons sugar,
1 cup mascarpone, $\frac{1}{2}$ cup cold green tea,
About 12 ladyfingers, Powdered sugar

Rinse lemon, dry thoroughly and grate zest. Beat egg yolk with sugar until creamy. Gradually stir in mascarpone, lemon peel and 3 tablespoons of green tea.

Depending on the size of the cups, cut ladyfingers into small pieces and form a layer in the bottom. Drizzle with green tea. Add a little egg mixture and top with another layer of ladyfingers soaked with tea. Top with remaining egg mixture and dust with a thick layer of powdered sugar. Cover cups with plastic wrap and refrigerate for at least 4 hours. Just before serving, dust with more powdered sugar.

🌿 Mix rum into the tea and soak the ladyfingers in a rum-tea mixture for an added punch.

Chestnut Spaghetti on Plum Soup

A heavenly and sumptuous dessert that will please everyone, served with a cup of green tea or with weak black tea and lime wedges.

> 1 cup peeled chestnuts (may also be canned or frozen), 1/2 cup milk, 1 1/2 cups cream, 3 tablespoons sugar, 2 tablespoons sugar, 1 teaspoon vanilla
> For the plum soup: 1 pound plums,
> 1 cup red wine, 3 tablespoons sugar, 1/2 cinnamon stick, Juice from 1/2 orange, Powdered sugar

Cut an X into the shells of the fresh chestnuts and bake in the oven at 400°F until they open slightly (about 15 minutes). Peel and cut into smaller pieces. If you used canned or frozen, simply cut them up.

In a saucepan, combine chestnuts, milk, cream, sugar and vanilla. Bring to a boil and then simmer for about 20–25 minutes while stirring occasionally until tender.

In the meantime, make plum soup. Rinse plums and remove pits. Combine plums, red wine, sugar, cinnamon and orange juice. Bring to a boil, then let stand for 10 minutes. Remove cinnamon stick and set aside. In a blender, purée chestnut mixture. Transfer slightly cooled plum soup to 4 soup bowls. Put chestnut mixture through a spaetzle press, letting it drop into the soup or spoon it into a pastry bag and pipe onto the soup as "spaghetti." Serve dusted with powdered sugar.

Red Tea Gelatin with Oranges

1 cup cold black tea, 1 cup red wine,
3 tablespoons sugar, $1/2$ cinnamon stick,
2 whole cloves, Juice from $1/2$ lemon,
6 leaves white gelatin, 2 oranges

In a saucepan, combine black tea, red wine, sugar, cinnamon, cloves and lemon juice. Simmer over very low heat for 5 minutes.

In the meantime, soften gelatin in cold water according to package directions. Peel oranges so that the white outer membrane is also removed and cut segments from between the inner membranes. Remove cinnamon stick and cloves from tea-red wine mixture. Squeeze out gelatin, dissolve completely in the warm liquid and let cool.

Distribute orange segments in chilled dessert glasses and add cold liquid. Refrigerate and let gel completely.

🌿 An ideal dessert for hot summer days, after a heavy meal or simply as an accompaniment with afternoon tea.

Savory Snacks and Dishes— Made or Served with Tea

You don't have to go to the London Savoy, the Paris Ritz or The Plaza in New York to enjoy an authentic five o'clock tea. Here are four delicious sandwich ideas you can make at home.

Cucumber Sandwiches with Tuna

1 small can tuna in water, $\frac{1}{2}$ cup mayonnaise,
Salt, Freshly ground white pepper,
Several drops Worcestershire sauce,
$\frac{1}{2}$ small cucumber, 8 slices sandwich bread

Drain tuna. Combine tuna and mayonnaise in a bowl and purée with a hand blender. Season with salt, pepper and Worcestershire sauce. Peel cucumber and slice thinly.

Remove crusts from bread and top 4 slices with cucumber. Spread with tuna mixture, top with remaining cucumber slices, then with remaining 4 bread slices. Press together firmly and cut in half diagonally.

Roast Beef Sandwiches

4 leaves iceberg lettuce, 8 slices sandwich bread,
$\frac{1}{2}$ cup horseradish cream (from a jar),
8 slices thinly sliced roast beef,
2 tablespoons Cumberland sauce (from a jar)

Rinse lettuce leaves and pat dry. Remove crusts from bread. Spread horseradish cream on 4 bread slices then top with lettuce leaves. Place 2 slices roast beef on each and spread with Cumberland sauce. Top with remaining bread slices and press together firmly. Cut in half diagonally.

Carrot Stilton Sandwiches

1 large carrot, 4 leaves head lettuce,
8 ounces Stilton (English blue cheese),
8 slices sandwich bread,
$\frac{1}{2}$ cup orange marmalade

Peel carrots and grate finely. Rinse lettuce leaves, pat dry and cut into fine strips. Cut Stilton into thin slices. Remove crusts from bread and spread with a thin layer of orange marmalade. Sprinkle 4 slices with grated carrot, top with cheese slices, then sprinkle with remaining grated carrot. Top with remaining bread slices with the marmalade side down and press together firmly. Cut in half diagonally.

Salmon Sandwiches

$^1/_3$ pound smoked salmon, sliced,
$^1/_2$ cup cream, 2 tablespoons whiskey,
Freshly ground white pepper, Freshly grated nutmeg,
$^2/_3$ cup heavy cream, 8 slices sandwich bread

Using a food processor, chop $^1/_2$ pound smoked salmon very finely. In a bowl, combine chopped salmon and cream, then put through a fine strainer. Stir in whiskey and season with pepper and nutmeg. Fold in heavy cream. Spread 4 bread slices with salmon cream and top with remaining salmon slices. Top with remaining bread slices and press together. Cut in half diagonally.

Royal Tea Butter

In general, Austrians call commercial butter "tea butter." Here's why: In 1906, Austria was commissioned to create a special butter for the English court that would be highly suitable for five o'clock tea. The British found Austrian sweet cream butter to be excellent, ensuring its future export. Austrian tea butter is available in any gourmet shop, but you can also make it yourself as follows:

Makes ½ pound fresh butter

4 cups non-pasteurized, whole milk,
2 tablespoons buttermilk to ⅓ cup cream

Pour milk into a wide bowl and let stand at 53–57°F for 10 hours or overnight. During this time, the milk will separate into cream and nonfat milk. Remove cream settled on the surface with a skimmer. For further processing, treat it with lactic acid bacteria as follows: In a bowl, pour 2 tablespoons buttermilk onto $1/3$ cup cream. Stir and let stand at about 68°F for at least 24 hours. The cream should become sour and thick.

Turn this thick mixture into butter by processing the fat globules into a smooth mixture through continuous beating. Using an electric mixer on the lowest setting, beat cream for 20–30 minutes. Drop the bowl of finished butter onto the work surface several times to release any trapped air bubbles. Chill thoroughly. Serve with tea accompanied by fresh bread or special crackers.

🍃 Although it's possible to make butter with an electric mixer, it's much easier if you have a special butter churn.

Wontons with Shiitake Mushrooms and Leeks

For the dough: ½ cup flour, 1 medium egg,
Approximately 3 tablespoons lukewarm water, Salt
For the filling: 5 dried shiitake mushrooms,
2 leeks, 1 tablespoon rice wine,
2 tablespoons soy sauce, Freshly ground pepper,
Sesame oil (as desired)

For the dough: On a floured work surface, knead together flour, egg, water and salt into a smooth and pliable dough. Wrap in a damp cloth or plastic wrap and let stand at room temperature for about 30 minutes.

For the filling: Place shiitakes in a bowl, pour boiling water over the top and let stand for 20 minutes. Cut leeks in half lengthwise, rinse between the leaves, remove most of the green parts and dice the rest finely. Squeeze liquid out of mushrooms and chop finely. Combine mushrooms, leeks, rice wine, soy sauce, pepper and sesame oil.

On a work surface, knead pasta dough thoroughly and roll out into a thin sheet. Using a pastry wheel, cut into rectangles of about 2 x 3 inches. Place 1–2 teaspoonfuls of filling in the center of each rectangle. Bring the dough edges together to form small packets. Carefully press wontons onto the work surface to give them a flat base so they will stand up.

Fill a wok or steamer pot one-third full of water and bring to a boil. Place wontons in a bamboo basket lined with a damp cloth or set inside a steamer insert. Place prepared insert in the wok or pot, cover with a lid and steam wontons for about 10 minutes.

 Serve wontons just as they're served in their native China—with "cha" (green tea).

 Serve wontons in the bamboo basket or on a large platter with dips on the side, such as prepared plum, oyster or sweet-and-sour sauce.

Variation: For Wontons with Turkey and Shrimp: Dice $\frac{1}{3}$ pound turkey and purée in a blender with 1–2 tablespoons rice wine. Clean and finely chop 1 stalk celery, 2 green onions and 1 small carrot. In a bowl, combine turkey mixture, chopped vegetables, $\frac{1}{4}$ pound peeled, chopped shrimp and 1 egg yolk. Add 2–3 tablespoons soy sauce, $\frac{1}{2}$ teaspoon sugar and 1 teaspoon sesame oil. Make wontons as described above using this filling.

Buddha's Vegetable Joy
with Butter Tea

The 14th Dalai Lama and Buddhist leader Tenzin Gyatso loved to drink butter tea. Whenever he stayed in a hotel, no matter where he was in the world, he would have hot water and a little butter brought to his room every hour. We don't know exactly what tea leaves he used, but it was probably green tea.

A touch of butter in tea does you good, calms the body and spirit, and tastes fantastic. I recommend serving it with a vegetable stir-fry:

$1/2$ pound bean sprouts, 2 carrots,
1 bell pepper, $1/2$ pound Chinese cabbage,
1 clove garlic, $1/2$ cup peanut oil,
$1/2$ pound diced tofu,
Salt, Freshly ground pepper,
2 tablespoons soy sauce,
2 tablespoons hoisin sauce,
$1/3$ cup vegetable stock

Rinse and drain bean sprouts. Peel or clean carrots. Cut bell peppers in half and remove stem, seeds and interior. Separate cabbage into leaves, rinse and pat dry. Cut carrots, bell pepper and Chinese cabbage into narrow strips. Peel garlic and dice finely.

In a wok or pan, heat half the peanut oil, sear diced tofu on all sides and remove. Add remaining peanut oil into wok and stir-fry vegetables for 5–8 minutes. Season with salt, pepper, soy sauce and hoisin sauce, then drizzle with vegetable stock. Carefully fold in tofu and add seasoning to taste.

Vary the vegetables depending on what's in season.

Marbled Tea Eggs from China

4 large white eggs, 3 tablespoons green tea leaves,
1 tablespoon salt, 1 teaspoon five-spice powder

Place eggs in a saucepan of cold water and bring to a boil. When the water starts to boil, simmer for about 6 minutes, stirring occasionally. Drain and rinse under cold water for several minutes. Carefully roll eggs on a work surface while exerting slight pressure until the shells crack.

Bring about 6 cups of water to a boil. Stir in tea leaves, salt and five-spice powder. Using a slotted spoon, place eggs in the tea water and let stand over low heat for about 30 minutes. Remove pan from heat, cover and leave eggs in water overnight.

On the following day, remove eggs from tea water, peel and cut into quarters. Arrange on a platter.

🍃 These nicely marbled eggs go with prepared Chinese sauces such as oyster and chili sauce.

🍃 Chinese five-spice powder typically comprises fennel, cinnamon, cloves, star anise and Szechwan pepper. It's available in most supermarkets.

Swiss Cheese Fondue

1 clove garlic, 14 ounces Gruyère,
7 ounces Emmenthaler, Juice from 1/2 lemon,
1 1/2 tablespoons cherry brandy (optional),
1 cup dry white wine, 2 tablespoons flour,
Freshly ground, coarse white pepper,
1 pinch freshly grated nutmeg,
1 crispy baguette, cut into bite-sized pieces

Peel garlic, cut in half and rub around the inside of a fondue pot. Dice both types of cheese finely and place in a nonstick saucepan. Add lemon juice, cherry brandy (if desired) and white wine. Melt slowly while stirring. Stir flour in a little water until smooth and use to thicken the cheese mixture. Transfer to the fondue pot and place on a heated tabletop burner. Season with pepper and nutmeg. Spear bread cubes with fondue forks and dig in!

🍃 Vary the fondue with other varieties of cheese such as Vacherin and Appenzeller. Seek advice from a cheese seller you trust.

🍃 Drinking black tea with cheese fondue makes it much easier to digest and renders the obligatory digestif unnecessary. But sometimes it's still nice to enjoy a little drop...

Little Tea Glossary

Auctions • Price negotiations based on supply and demand take place on a regular basis in producing countries. Even at trans-shipment sites such as Antwerp, London and Amsterdam, "tea exchanges" hold auctions.

Black tea blends • Almost all commercially available teas are blends of several varieties. The different ratios within the blends are intended to compensate for fluctuations in quality and price. An East Frisian blend, for example, is a hearty black tea blend containing Assam, Ceylon, Java or Sumatra teas. An English blend, on the other hand, usually contains Darjeeling, Assam and Ceylon.

Blends • See black tea blends.

Broken • Tea leaves chopped in a "cutter" or rolled, reducing leaf size.

Caffeine • This alkaloid is responsible for tea's stimulating effect; also called theine.

Cultivating countries • The tea plant grows in regions with a tropical and temperate climate, plenty of precipitation and lots of sunshine. The principal countries are Bangladesh, China, india (in the Darjeeling, Assam and Doars Provinces), Japan, Malaysia, Singapore, Sri Lanka, Tibet and Vietnam.

Cutter • A cutter is the machine that chops processed leaves to make "broken" varieties.

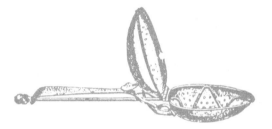

Darjeeling • The finest highland teas come from this northern Indian province.

Dull • Tea is designated as dull when it does not have a "clear" aroma.

Dust • The smallest grade of tea, mainly used in tea bags.

Fannings • Leaf particles that have been sifted out of larger grades and quickly give infusions a deep color. Because of this property, fannings are added to other grades or used in teabag production.

Fermentation • Freshly picked tea leaves are first crushed in a roller to break up the leaf cells and release the cell sap. The leaf sap then reacts with oxygen in the air to form the aroma, break down tannins and turn leaves a copper color. The fermented leaves are then dried with hot air, giving black tea its characteristic coloring.

Flavored teas • Black or green teas are flavored by adding flavorings, peels, blossoms, leaves or spices. Tea shops offer an endless selection of flavored teas in a wide range of flavors, including pineapple, mango, apple, peach and cinnamon. A popular example of tea flavored with blossoms is jasmine tea.

Fluff • Refers to fine dust generated during tea production. The fluff is discarded.

Flush • A complete, new growth of leaves and buds on a tea plant. This term also refers to the picking (harvesting) of these shoots.

Flush, first • The first tea leaves picked in a year, sometimes with the name of the cultivation region added (e.g. First Flush Darjeeling). The infusion has a pleasantly mild, delicately tart aroma.

Flush, second • The second harvest. Top quality leaves that result in infusions with a super-spicy aroma.

Green tea • For this tea, the leaves are steamed (Japan) or roasted (China) but not fermented, which is why they retain their green color.

Herbal infusions • Fruit and herb teas such as peppermint, chamomile, fennel, rosehip, lime blossom and valerian. Mate tea, which also falls into this category, is made from the leaves of the Brazilian mate plant (extremely stimulating).

High grown • Tea with a distinctive aroma from highland tea-growing regions. Tea from the Darjeeling province, for example, grows in the Himalayan foothills at altitudes of up to 8000 feet.

Leaf tea • Only about two percent of world production is leaf tea. The leaves are kept largely intact during processing. This means that very little liquid is released from the tea leaves, giving the infusion a light and aromatic flavor. Unbroken varieties are almost exclusively from Darjeeling.

Oolong • Semi-fermented tea that is somewhere between black tea and green tea. It has a light aroma and a golden color.

Orange pekoe • A grade of large, whole leaf tea.

Pekoe • Young, tender tea leaves, from the Chinese for "white down." Pekoes produce a strong infusion.

Processed tea drinks • This category includes tea extracts, instant tea products, decaffeinated tea and iced tea. Commercially available iced teas contain at least 0.12 percent tea extract.

Souchong • The Chinese name for the coarsest grade, with little aroma and producing a weak infusion.

Tea extracts • Dried, powdered extracts from tea leaves. In their commercially available form, they are generally over-sweetened and contain flavor additives such as lemon or other fruits.

Tea liqueur • Fancy, finely flavored liqueur with minimum 25 percent vol. alcohol. Japan also produces a green tea liqueur.

Teaspoon • Internationally recognized unit of measure, but also a symbolic object for tea lovers.

Tea taster • As with coffee, most teas comprise a blend of different varieties. Because annual harvests differ in terms of quality and flavor, tea tasters are employed to detect these differences and put together balanced blends. Many tea tasters taste up to 500 samples per day!

TGFOP • Abbreviation for "tippy golden flowery orange pekoe" leaves. The name applies only to Darjeeling teas with a large proportion of young, tender tea leaves that have little cell juice, and, therefore, are not darkened by fermentation.

Tipp • Refers to a tea plant with a large number of young leaf tips (which are low in tannins).

White tea • This tea comes mainly from China. The fresh tea leaves are neither fermented, steamed or roasted, they are simply air-dried.

List of Recipes

Teas & Punches—
Hot and Stimulating

Iced Teas & Mixed Drinks—
Cool and Refreshing

Cakes & Pastries—
Made or Served with Tea

Jellies & Desserts—
Sweet and Fruity

Savory Snacks and Dishes— Made or Served with Tea